C0-BEG-637

PROTECTED LANDSCAPE AREA

Biele Karpaty • Cerová vrchovina • Horná Orava • Kysuce • Latorica •
Malé Karpaty • Muránska planina • Poľana • Ponitrie • Slovenský kras •
Strážovské vrchy • Štiavnické vrchy • Veľká Fatra • Vihorlat •
Východné Karpaty • Záhorie

CURATIVE AND MINERALS SPRINGS

Bardejovské Kúpele • Bojnice • Brusno • Číž • Dudince • Korytnica •
Kováčová • Lúčky • Nimnica • Piešťany • Rajecké Teplice • Sklené Teplice •
Sliač • Smrdáky • Trenčianske Teplice • Turčianske Teplice • Vyšné Ružbachy

CAVES

Belianska • Bystrianska • Demänovská jaskyňa Slobody • Demänovská ľadová •
Dobšinská ľadová • Domica • Driny • Gombasecká • Harmanecká • Jasovská •
Ochtinská aragonitová • Važecká

Slovakia

Eugen Lazišťan
Fedor Mikovič
Ivan Kučma

English translator
Anna Jurečková

BOLCHAZY-CARDUCCI PUBLISHERS, INC.

Slovakia
A Photographic Odyssey

VYDAVATEĽSTVO NEOGRAFIE • MARTIN

THIS BOOK IS MADE POSSIBLE BY
The Slovak-American International Cultural
Foundation, Inc.

2001 Reprint
Bolchazy-Carducci Publishers, Inc.
1000 Brown St., Unit 101
Wauconda, IL 60084 USA
http://www.bolchazy.com
ISBN 0-86516-517-3

and

© 2001 Vydavateľstvo Neografie, Martin
ISBN 80-88892-23-6

Compiled by
EUGEN LAZIŠŤAN

Photographs: K. Belický, P. Brenkus, E. Čeňková, K. Demuth, L. Deneš,
D. Dugas, P. Havran, O. Hraško, A. Jiroušek, L. Jiroušek,
✝ E. Jurisa, J. Krátky, D. Kusák, F. Lašut, E. Lazišťan,
M. Lichner, Š. Marton, B. Molnár, J. Pavelek, ✝ K. Plicka,
J. Procházka, J. Sláma, D. Slivka,
✝ F. Spáčil, F. Šlachta, M. Tesák
End leaves Ondrej Hraško
Graphic layout by Veronika Kramárová, Robert Brož
Text Fedor Mikovič
Editor-in-chief Ivan Kučma
Translation Anna Jurečková
Published and printed by Neografia, a. s.,
Škultétyho 1, 036 55 Martin, Slovak Republic

Front cover photo: Bratislava Castle
Back cover photo: Break of dawn above Kriváň
Title double-page: Kriváň
Page 5: Devín Castle

Library of Congress Cataloging-in-Publication Data

Lazistan, Eugen.
    Slovakia: a photographic odyssey / Eugen Lazistan, Fedor Mikovic, Ivan Kucma;
English translator Anna Jurecková.
        p. cm.
    ISBN 0-86516-517-3
    1. Slovakia--Pictorial works. I. Mikovic, Fedor. II. Kucma, Ivan. III. Title.

DB2713 .L39 2001
943.73--dc21
                                                                                2001025084

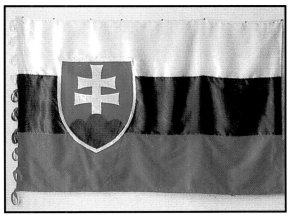

THE STATE ANTHEM OF THE SLOVAK REPUBLIC

NAD TATROU SA BLÝSKA

Nad Tatrou sa blýska hromy divo bijú
Zastavme ich bratia
Veď sa ony stratia
Slováci ožijú.

To Slovensko naše posiaľ tvrdo spalo
Ale blesky hromu
Vzbudzujú ho k tomu
Aby sa prebralo

JANKO MATÚŠKA

FROM THE TATRAS TO THE DANUBE spreads the charming country whose name is Slovakia. Specialists in tourism say that this small spot on the Earth in the centre of Europe occupying an area of only 49,030 square kilometres can boast thirty-seven assets for tourism. Just the thirty-eighth one is missing – the sea. The substitutes for it are natural thermal springs with well-equipped resort centres built

around them. Let us list at least the most famous ones: Štúrovo, Dunajská Streda, Komárno, Patince, Čalovo, Margita-Ilona, Santovka, Tornaľa, Bešeňová, Liptovský Ján, Oravice.

The world-renowned spa resorts such as Piešťany, Turčianske Teplice, Sliač, but also those of Bardejov, Kováčová, Rajecké Teplice, Dudince, Číž, Smrdáky, Brusno and others cannot be omitted from this list. Springs of health and life are scattered across all of Slovakia forming an amazingly rich mineral necklace consisting of 1,200 thermal springs.

Large mountains belong to the most precious jewels of Slovakia. They are part of the Carpathians extending in more than a 1,400-km long line from Bratislava as far as to the Black Sea. In their mighty arch, it is especially the High Tatras that attract attention, superb mountains 26 kilometres long, and, on average, only 17 kilometres wide. They are called "the smallest giant mountains of the world". Amidst their three hundred peaks, the highest one – 2,655-m high Gerlachovský Štít – touches the clouds. Not far away from it towers the most beautiful 2,494-m high Slovak mountain Kriváň, symbol of freedom and independence of all the citizens of the Slovak Republic. It was declared independent on Jan. 1, 1993. Its population is 5.3 million including the Slovaks (85.6%), Hungarians (10.8%), Romanies (1.5%), Ukranians (0.3%), Ruthenians (0.3%), Germans and Poles.

The first people settled in the territory of present Slovakia as early as one hundred thousand years ago, in the Paleolithic Era. The oldest evidence of human existence in our territory is 120 thousand years old – it is a travertine moulding of the skull of a Neanderthal man found at Gánovce near Poprad.

The oldest children's toy, a toy-cart model dating back to the Bronze Age, was found in a child's grave at Nižná Myšľa near Košice. Nothing similar has been found in other parts of Europe. Here have been unearthed the most numerous archeological finds documenting the Otoman people's culture, about 1,600 years B.C.E.

An even older artifact is Venus of Moravany, an inconspicuous 7-cm tall statuette found at Moravany near Piešťany in 1967. A prehistoric artist carved it from a mammoth tusk more than 22 thousand years ago.

According to the archeological finds unearthed in Bratislava, the oldest stone building in present Slovakia's territory dates back to the Bronze Age and is the work of the Celts. It was they who introduced money here as early as the beginning of the 2nd century B.C.E. Inscriptions on the Celtic coins bearing the names of their princes are the first known texts discovered in this territory. The most frequent coin inscription is *Biatec*. The Celtic coin discovery in Bratislava is the largest one in Central Europe.

After the Celts, shortly before the Christian era, the Romans penetrated as far north as the Danube River and, to protect their "eternal" empire, they made use of not only the mighty flow of the river but also of a clever fortification complex called *limes Romanus*. It consisted of the military forts in Rusovce, Bratislava, Štúrovo and Komárno. The inscription marked by them after the Marcoman wars in 179 C.E. on the Trenčín Castle rock is a monumental epigraph documenting the presence of the Roman legions of the emperors Marcus Aurelius and Commodus in the town encampment called Laugaricio. It was written to remind future generations of their victory over the Quads. Slovakia has become a part of world literature: on the banks of the River Hron, Marcus Aurelius wrote his excellent work *Talks to Myself (Meditations)*.

The Slavs started to come to this part of Europe during the 4th and 5th centuries establishing small agricultural settlements. But it was as late as the 15th century when they started to call their homeland Slovakia. It was in those times when the word Slovak appeared for the first time. Spelled as *Zlowachko* it can be found on the pages of the first Hungarian chronicler Ján from Turiec. In 1488, he published his work, *Chronica Hungarorum,* one of the biggest and greatest chronicles ever printed in Hungary.

Academia Istropolitana, the first university, was founded in 1465 in Bratislava, the present capital of the Slovak Republic with a population of 450,000. Trnava, located not far away from Bratislava, is on the other hand the oldest Slovak town. It was granted freedom and privileges of royal towns in 1238. However, the first Slovak ruler – Prince Pribina – had his seat in Nitra; its first record comes from the year 826. In 623 Frank merchant Samo founded the first historically confirmed Slavonic state right in the territory of the present Slovak Republic. It was later transformed into Greater Moravia, but at the turn of the 9th and 10th centuries, it succumbed to the invasions of the Magyar tribes. In Arpad Hungary, a new state founded in the Carpathian basin in the 10th century, the Slavonic population was exposed to new domination.

During the 13th and 14th centuries, under the reign of the Arpads and Anjous, trading and mining towns started to grow and develop. The late-Gothic culture of the royal mining centres, especially those of Banská Bystrica, Kremnica, Banská Štiavnica, Ľubietová, and Nová Baňa, ranked the territory of Slovakia with the richest European regions of those times. Speaking about wealth, the oldest mint in Europe is that in Kremnica. It was founded in 1328 in the vicinity of the world-famous Kremnica gold deposits. Besides Hungarian groschen or golden florens, here were also minted famous Kremnica ducats considered the most respected and valuable money in medieval Europe. In 1627 here at Bieberštôlňa (gallery), gunpowder was used for the first time not for military purposes but to blast gold and silver-bearing ore. In 1762 Banská Štiavnica achieved another primacy – the first mining university in the world was established here.

No wonder this historical town together with the mountain village Vlkolinec near Ružomberok and the Spiš Castle, (12th century, the largest castle in Central Europe – 4.1 hectares), are on the UNESCO list of the world's cultural heritage. Some fortified classical buildings in Slovakia are also connected with European culture: great Beethoven composed some of his works in the mansion at Dolná Krupá (his „Moonlight Sonata" is said to be composed there) and Franz Schubert in the mansion at Želiezovce. The masterpiece of film expressionism, *Nosferatu* (1921), directed by F. W. Murnau was shot at the Orava Castle and its vicinity.

The rich history of the country lying under the Tatras is documented in numerous cultural and historical sights. They include 10 folk architecture reservations, up to 90 museums, 20 galleries, 425 mansions, 98 castles and a chateaux. The oldest one of them is Devín Castle, positioned at the confluence of the Morava and Danube Rivers. Archeologists have documented the Devín Castle settlements since the 5th century B.C.E.

Slovakia has also sacred historical sights. One of the most magnificent is the Church of St. Elizabeth in Košice built in late-Gothic style at the turn of the 14th and 15th centuries. It is not only the most significant Gothic building in Slovakia but also the eastern-most situated structure of its kind in Europe.

Among the Bratislava churches, Concathedral of St. Martin is ranked at the top. Besides its Gothic architecture, attention is attracted also by its bronze Gothic baptismal font from 1403 as well as its fine woodcarving and painting decorations. It was also for their beauty that Hungarian kings chose the Church of St. Martin as their coronation site. And it was in this church on June 15th, 1999, that the glorious Te Deum resounded on the occasion of the inauguration ceremony for the first President of the Slovak Republic elected directly by its citizens. Rudolf Schuster was their choice.

The masterpiece of Master Paul, one of the greatest woodcarvers in medieval Europe, is definitely worth mentioning as a church attraction. It is the main Gothic altar in the Church of St. James in Levoča containing splendidly carved decorations. The artist finished it in 1517. Its height of 18.62 m makes it one of the tallest wooden wing altars of the world.

The highest located settlement is Štrbské Pleso, a well known recreational sports and health centre built at a height of 1335 metres. On the other hand, the lowest place is in the south of Slovakia where the Bodrog River leaves the republic territory, near the small town of Streda nad Bodrogom. Its height is only 94 metres. Not far away from there – in Slovenský Kras (karst) – is the deepest gorge, called Brázda (205 metres).

Except for fertile Danube lowland in the southwest and East Slovak lowland in the southeast (altogether covering 22 percent of the state area), the rest of its surface constitutes mountains and basins. Speleologists discovered more than 3,800 caves inside them; 12 of them are open to the public.

Here is our ranking of caves. Dobšinská Ice Cave is the largest (and according to the specialists, also the most richly decorated) ice cave in Europe. Inside, there are 145,000 cubic metres of ice. In 1896, it was equipped with electricity as the first one in the world.

In Slovakia, these natural jewels are protected in 370 nature reservations covering more than one sixth of the state territory. In addition, Slovakia is under professional environmental protection in another 16 protected areas and 5 national parks.

The mountainous surface of Slovakia has an impact on its climate; it is mild and continental. The warmest place in Slovakia is Štúrovo, the town located in the area where the Danube leaves Slovak territory; its average temperatures is +10 °C. The coldest place in Slovakia is the top of the mountain Lomnický Štít (2632 m) with an average temperature of –3.7 °C.

Large woods and forests contribute to the country's beauty and wealth and have beneficial effects on man's physical and mental health. They cover 37 percent of its area ranking it 4th among the most wooded countries in Europe. Spruce forests constitute one fourth of all forests.

The Danube is the largest river crossing Slovak territory with a length of 22.5 km (forming Slovak-Austrian and Slovak-Hungarian boundaries in its 149-kilometre course). Its flow in Bratislava reaches 200 thousand cubic metres per second. Beyond Bratislava, the Lesser Danube splits from the main course forming Žitný ostrov (island) with an area of 1,600 square kilometres, the largest river island in Europe. It is our biggest source of underground waters.

Our wandering around remarkable and exceptional landmarks of Slovakia has only started. We hope that this book will make you set out on a journey to search for knowledge and beauty. Dear readers, on behalf of all its authors, I wish you many unforgettable experiences.

Fedor Mikovič

◁◁ Bratislava and the Danube, view from Petržalka
◁ Bratislava Castle, the dominant of the capital of the Slovakia
   Bratislava, St. Martin's Concathedral and its immediate vicinity, view
   from the castle

Bratislava, Roland's Fountain and the tower of Old Town Hall

Bratislava, Grassalkovich Palace – today the seat of the President   Bratislava, roccocco House At the Good Shepherd's

Bratislava, building of Slovak Parliament
Bratislava, Slovak Republic Government Office building

Bratislava, Primatial Palace by Melchior Hefele

Bratislava, the City Redoute – concert of the Slovak Philharmonics' Choir

Bratislava, Slovak National Theatre – opera Svätopluk by Eugen Suchoň

Bratislava, Michalská Street with St. Michael's Gate

Bratislava, arcade passageway of the Old Town Hall

Wheel watermill on the Lesser Danube at Tomášikovo

Brhlovce, rock dwellings carved in tuff walls

Gabčíkovo, monumental dam on the Danube

Červený Kameň, view of the southwestern wing of the main castle palace

Červený Kameň, sala terrena on the ground floor of the ceremonial wing of the castle

Nitra, entrance gate to the outer fortification wall of the Castle

Nitra, main altar of the castle Church – Descent from the Cross by Pernegger

Beckov Castle, early Gothic castle tower on a seep cliff   Ruins of Čachtice Castle, entrance to the outer castle walls

Piešťany, balneological centre Thermia Palace amidst flowers and greenery

Piešťany, covered colonnade bridge across the Váh River

Trenčianske Teplice, spa house Sina with Hamman bath built in the Oriental style

Trenčianske Teplice, balneological centre Krym and hotel Jalta in the centre of the resort

Trenčín, the neoromantic building of the renewed synagogue.   Castle of Trenčín, view of the westernside with Luis's Palace

Čičmany, Radena's house with gallery and characteristic ornamental decoration

Embroidering women from Čičmany wearing beautiful folk dress

Žilina, Jesuits' church and cloister on historical Mariánske Square

Meander of the Váh River at Domašín with a view of Malá Fatra range

Strečno, ruins of medieval watch castle and the Váh Valley

Martin, front of the first building of Matica slovenská, today it houses Slovak National Literary Museum – National Culture Memorial of Matica slovenská

Martin, Theatre of the Slovak National Uprising (Studio)
Martin, exhibition of the Slovak National Literary Museum at National Hall

◁ Kremnica, main square with plaque column, some burghers' houses and castle church in the backgroud
Chateau of Bojnice, one of the most frequently visited landmarks

Chateau of Bojnice, interior of the Golden Hall, the main ceremonial hall of the chateau

Banská Štiavnica, Old Castle – historical dominat of the town, view from the south

Banská Bystrica, panoramatic view of the historical Square of Slovak National Uprising with historical buildings ▷

Hronský Beňadik, portal of the Romanesque Basilika of St. Benedict

Liptovská Štiavnica, late Renaissance chateau, originally with two towers, later rebuilt to a four-tower structure

Likava Castle, ancient stronghold of feudal power, is today only a tourist attraction

Tvrdošín, wooden Gothic church (on the UNESCO list of cultural heritage)

Orava Castle, general view from the Orava River

Western Tatras – Roháče, view of the Tri kopy ridge from the lake Štvrté pleso

Western Tatras – Roháče, steep climb to Plačlivô Peak

The Low Tatras, rocky formation The Window over Jánska Valley

The Low Tatras, rocky massif of Ďumbier, the highest peak in the range

Jaskyňa slobody (Cave of Freedom) at Demänová, Hall of Miracles with rich stalagmite and stalactite decorations

Jaskyňa slobody (Cave of Freedom) at Demänová, Big Temple with water-lily pond

The High Tatras, Temnosmrečinská Valley

The High Tatras, Kriváň with the Belá River, view from Podbanské

The High Tatras, Malý Ľadový and Ľadový peaks, view from
Kolový peak

The High Tatras ridges, view from Gerlachovský Peak westward

Pieniny range, the Dunajec River at Lesnica with Sokolice massif in the background

Rafting down the Dunajec River in the fault of the Dunajec, inseparable attraction of Pieniny range

Levoča, main altar by Master Paul in St. James's church, the tallest wooden Gothic altar in Europe

Levoča, St. James's church and Renaissance town hall with oriels, main dominants in the Old town centre

◁ Panoramatic view of Spiš Castle and Spišská Kapitula
Žehra, ancient early Gothic church with precious interior, after later
building adaptations

Spišská Kapitula, twin-tower late Romanesque Basilica of St. Martin

Dobšinská Ice Cave, bizarre ice formations of different shapes in Veľká   Slovenský raj (Slovak Paradise), Veľký Sokol (Big Falcon), ice falls at

Košice, St. Elizabeth's Church, the most important Gothic architectural monument in Slovakia

Košice, Dominican Church, Gothic in its origin, after later Baroque adaptations

Prešov, Renaissance burgher's houses – the Rákoci House in the right
Medzilaborce, Museum of Modern Art, Andy Warhol
exhibition

Košice, an evening-view of the restored theatre

Bardejov, restored Thick Bastion, part of the town fortification

Bardejov, view of the monumental Gothic altar from the chancel in St. Egid's Church

Jasov, late Baroque twin-tower structure of church with cloister

Jasov, mural paintings by J. L. Kracker inside the cloister

Krásna Hôrka, panorama of the castle towering above Krásnohorské
Podhradie on steep conical hill ▷
Košice, singing fountain ▷▷